HAROLD KLEMP

THE SPIRITUAL LIFE

HAROLD KLEMP

ECKANKAR
Minneapolis
www.Eckankar.org

ABOUT THIS BOOK: *The Spiritual Life* is compiled from Harold Klemp's writings. These selections originally appeared in his books published by Eckankar.

The Spiritual Life

Printed in USA
Compiled by Joan Klemp
Edited by Patrick Carroll, Joan Klemp, and Anthony Moore
Cover photo by Jim Brandenberg/Minden Pictures
Author photo by Robert Huntley
Cover design by Doug Munson

Library of Congress Cataloging-in-Publication Data

Klemp, Harold.
   The spiritual life / Harold Klemp.
      p. cm.
   ISBN 978-1-57043-359-7 (hardcover : alk. paper)
   1. Spiritual life—Eckankar (Organization) 2. Eckankar (Organization)—Doctrines.   I. Title.
   BP605.E3K57435 2011
   299'.93—dc23

                                    2011020942

♾ This paper meets the requirements of ANSI/NISO Z39.48-1992 (Permanence of Paper).

CONTENTS

DEAR READER

We live in an unprecedented time of spiritual opportunity! You may say, With the world in such turmoil, can this be true?

Maybe we can't change the whole world, but we can change our part of it. We can awaken to the spiritual life by exploring the spiritual opportunities offered in this book.

We can change our perspective, our consciousness, and our relationship with the world like never before. "No matter what we were in the past during any other life," says the author, "we are spiritually greater today."

In *The Spiritual Life*, Harold Klemp's wisdom, insight, techniques, and inspiring contemplation seeds can help you change your world for the better. Take one quote each day and contemplate its meaning. You will find it easier and easier to see beyond turmoil and confusion and *live* the spiritual life every day.

$\mathcal{S}$OUL'S
AWAKENING

$\mathcal{L}$ife is a dream from beginning to end.

You are Soul, a particle of God sent into the worlds to gain spiritual experience.

*S*oul can be in several different places at the same time.

*M*ost people have hardly any idea about their life in the higher spiritual worlds while their body lies asleep at day's end.

*D*uring the process of waking up,
Soul is returning from these far places.

*T*he dream world and its people are real. It is only our recall and understanding of it that are incomplete.

*S*ome people naturally enjoy vivid recollections of their dream state, but those who don't can develop the skill.

*I*t is possible to develop a sharper recall of the dream state by keeping a notebook by the bed, with pen and light at hand.

Dreams tell how you are getting on with Divine Spirit and life.

*L*ike a daily report card, dreams show you how you are doing in your spiritual mission, even if you don't know you have one.

*S*oul's desire is conscious evolution.
Life always takes us forward if we will go.

SPIRITUAL PROTECTION

*P*eople all over the world ask how to navigate the perils and adventures of the spiritual life.

Divine Spirit opens up new opportunities, but we must take them.

You must make your own choices with the best information at hand. Only then can Spirit help and guide you.

*T*here are several means of protection to use against those who intrude into our state of being.

If psychic attacks bother us, it's because sometime in the past we have opened the door.

By adopting a different attitude about What will people think? we get better at handling the subtle pressures and guilts thrown at us.

A way to heal oneself begins with a spiritual exercise.

Singing HU, the sacred name for God, opens the channels of healing.

*H*U sounds like the word *hue,* but drawn out.

People sing HU quietly or aloud to receive protection from trouble or danger on the street, at work, or in the home.

The love and protection of the Holy Spirit, which we call the ECK, are with you in all spiritual concerns.

SOLVING
LIFE'S
PROBLEMS

*T*he path of ECK is not meant to finally end the succession of life's problems, for they are given as opportunities for Soul's unfoldment.

CK is an individual path, as is life.

*N*o two people are alike. Each has an agreement with life that is unlike any other.

As one develops the inner link with Divine Spirit, one's ability to take charge of his own life increases.

All problems come from the inner to the outer. The individual must be honest with himself.

*L*ife is truly meeting ourselves. The complaints we have of others are reflections of our own deficiencies.

When you ask for help, the ECK begins to bring changes that are for your good.

*B*efore Divine Spirit can make any changes, you must develop a better image of yourself.

*T*he spiritual exercises build up spiritual momentum for Soul to realize the godlike being that It is.

*O*ur detours are only so much learning. God cares only that Soul is perfected sometime in Its wanderings.

*E*ach problem we control takes us one step closer to self-mastery.

PAST LIVES

*N*o matter what we were in the past during any other life, we are spiritually greater today.

All conditions are due to karma.

A study of dreams can help people learn the spiritual reason their life is as it is, and what they can do to improve their lot.

*T*o awaken past-life dreams, make a note of things you greatly like or dislike. Then watch your dreams.

*K*eep a record of your dreams. Write a short note about every dream you recall upon awakening.

$\mathcal{A}$lso be alert during the day for clues about your problem from other people. The Holy Spirit works through them too. So be aware and listen.

The path of ECK is not for the God-Realized but for those who wish to reach that station—no matter what their starting point.

The past is past. The seeker of God practices the spiritual exercises and lives in the Sound and Light of Divine Spirit.

A simple spiritual exercise called The Easy Way is one way of opening to the more bountiful life of Spirit.

The way to do this is to close your eyes, look into your Spiritual Eye (above and between your eyebrows), and chant HU—a name for God. You can also chant *God* or another holy word. Try this for fifteen or twenty minutes a day.

If you let go and give your concerns to Divine Spirit, you will be guided to the best avenue to take next.

FAMILY RELATIONSHIPS

*P*ut full attention on the daily affairs in your life, for this is also part of that which touches the spiritual consciousness.

A true marriage has commitment by each person. Both realize the responsibility of that commitment.

A marriage of the heart lets each of the couple remain an individual, but the two are as one.

*B*e gentle and kind to yourself. We are all beginners in living.

Harmony in a family is a sacred thing.

To get in control of your anger, try to catch yourself in the middle of an argument. Then chant HU softly to yourself.

*I*t's hard to let our grown-up children learn the consequences of their own actions.

What hides behind attachment? The fear of loss.

What can overcome such fear? Divine love.

*T*he greatest thing we can possibly gain from this life is the ability to love, and to love greatly.

*E*CK enhances our life and gives insight, strength, and understanding where we found only darkness before.

*T*he teachings of ECK are to give us a deep spiritual healing that touches all aspects of our lives.

BALANCE AND HARMONY

The question is really, How do I open myself to life and still stay in balance?

*B*efore you can improve your life and find a measure of happiness, you must learn to do one thing every day out of pure love.

Giving, or outflow, serves to balance us in our daily life.

$\mathscr{P}$eople spiritually in balance do what they can to create a better life for themselves and their loved ones.

*T*he teachings of ECK are about us being willing to change our state of consciousness to something better.

When something appears to go wrong, look for the lesson in it for you, instead of finding fault with anyone else or even yourself.

*T*o avoid making karma, while either awake or asleep, sing HU. Sing it when you are angry, frightened, or alone.

*H*U calms and restores, because it sets your thoughts upon the highest spiritual ideal.

*N*othing is insurmountable for Soul; It learns how to make everything into stepping-stones instead of stumbling blocks.

Graceful living is to realize everything that comes into your life is for the
good.

As we put effort into bringing harmony and balance into our life, these efforts are enhanced by the ECK.

THE ROAD TO GOD

*S*oul exists because God loves It. Its destiny is to become a Co-worker with God.

*Y*ou are Soul. It is the real you.

You are a timeless, deathless spark of God—in love, strength, and beauty—upheld by the always present Light and Sound, the Holy Spirit.

A spiritual path ought to show the way to God. If you find one that does this, then follow it. If not, you must find another that fits you.

Divine Spirit has provided many paths for Soul to take back to God.

Earth is a training ground where Soul faces hard choices to pick what suits It now.

*H*ow are you going to make the best use of this life? How are you going to build toward an experience that is rich for Soul?

The answer is reflected in the only true mission of Soul: to become a citizen of the spiritual worlds while still in the physical worlds.

*T*he teachings of ECK are located within the heart. The key lies in the Spiritual Exercises of ECK, simple techniques that take only minutes a day.

*T*hey uplift Soul in Its state of consciousness and lead to the Light and Sound of God.

*L*earning the invisible laws that affect our every act, whether or not we are conscious of them, will allow us to straighten out our life.

We find that every aspect of our personal life begins to be smoother.

*W*hich path fits you best? Only you can answer that. Soul has got to find Its niche in the scheme of things.

CHANGE AND GROWTH

*L*ife teaches that all living beings go through cycles of change.

*S*oul operates in cycles of activity and rest. The ECK gives us choices that we accept and grow from.

*T*imes change, and so does the ability of people to perceive truth better.

Every Soul is a spark of God.

The path of ECK encourages the freedom and responsibility of Soul. That is Its birthright.

*D*ivine Spirit begins to straighten out the affairs of the individual who follows Its way. Yet It never hurries one.

The Spiritual Exercises of ECK are designed to expand one's consciousness at a pace that is comfortable.

*S*oul gathers an education in the lower worlds so It can become a true citizen in the spiritual community.

There comes a time when we realize that our efforts at unfoldment are only personal. Besides the Inner Master, no one can help us up the ladder to God.

The Inner Master, of course, is just the inner form of Spirit, of the ECK, Holy Spirit.

*T*he path of ECK is to let one develop spiritual stamina and become a Master in his own right.

This is the meaning of Co-worker with God.

CREATIVITY
AND
SELF-DISCIPLINE

*L*ife is acknowledged to be a stormy sea. Yet so often when the boat rocks we fly into a panic, as if a boat shouldn't rock in a storm.

The spiritual way teaches balance and moderation in all departments of living.

*M*ost important in the spiritual works of ECK is the knowledge that a solution to every problem is within us.

*S*ome habits are deeply ingrained. No one expects them to go away immediately.

Divine Spirit often begins working for our welfare after we have made some small effort first.

The human consciousness can act like a pit of quicksand. The Spiritual Exercises of ECK are a rope we can use to pull ourselves free.

It really makes very little difference what we choose to do with our talents and interests.

*W*hatever you plan to do, find something you really want to do—and are willing to sweat and labor for without recognition.

A person is obligated to do all he can for himself, but when his best efforts fail, then he turns the whole bundle over to Divine Spirit to see how it can be done the right way.

*N*o matter what outer events arise to throw us off our spiritual center, we must return to the Sound and Light of God.

*L*ook always to the Light and Sound of God within you, and you will always sail the cosmic sea of ECK.

SPIRITUAL GOALS

*S*oul is a joyful, creative, and active being.

We decide what we want to achieve in our lives, and then we make step-by-step goals to accomplish our ends.

You know your *general* purpose is to become a Co-worker with God. So how do you identify your *personal* goal?

We can serve as vehicles for Spirit by just being ourselves.

The individual must make an honest evaluation of his talents, interests, and training to decide what goals he wishes to strive for.

*E*ach activity contains within it the
seed of a spiritual lesson.

We must first give to life if we expect life to give anything in return. This is the divine law.

An unselfish dream, goal, or service can help us to the height of spiritual living.

*I*f the ECK brings a new direction into our life, which falls outside our original master plan, we contemplate upon it. We are willing to change our direction.

*E*ach person on the path of ECK has his choice, his free will.

*T*he ECK will bring you many right seasons for spiritual growth. Contemplate upon them.

$\mathscr{S}$OUL TRAVEL

The veil lifts gradually from our spiritual eyesight as we become ready to look farther into the spiritual realities.

*B*oth the dream state and Soul Travel are doors to the same spiritual worlds.

The dynamic kind of Soul Travel is unforgettable for anyone who is able to have it. It occurs through the practice of the Spiritual Exercises of ECK.

When going to bed for the night, you can simply say to the Inner Master: "I give you permission to take me where I am ready to go."

You cannot become lost in your own inner worlds, because the Far Country is your personal universe.

The Inner Master is simply there to acquaint you with your own worlds of being.

*E*ventually, science will catch up to the knowledge of those who already can explore the spiritual states of living beings by Soul Travel.

*T*oday the sailors of the cosmic sea are recording their journeys into the unknown world beyond the physical plane in their spiritual journals and in the books and articles they write.

*S*oul Travel brings Soul through the lower worlds—the Astral, Causal, Mental, and Etheric Planes—until one reaches the Soul Plane.

Here, one begins to work with seeing, knowing, and being. It is a whole new ball game.

*S*oul Travel may also come as an increased awareness and insight into everyday situations.

The ECK Masters work with the individual through the different planes in order to maintain balance in the physical, everyday life.

You do not have to Soul Travel to be successful in ECK. Another way to God-Realization is to give tender love and care to every action, because of your love for God.

THE
ECK MASTERS

*W*hen one steps onto the path of ECK, he is shown the reality of the ECK Masters.

*T*he ECK Masters are spiritual guides people have looked to since the beginning of time for guidance, protection, and divine love.

By the way, "ECK" means the Holy Spirit.

The ECK Masters are agents of God whose only concern is to bring spiritual upliftment to each individual ready for it.

*M*ostly they work behind the scenes. Yet the Living ECK Master's mission is a public one: to carry the ECK message to the people of the world.

*E*very person has a chance to find spiritual freedom. The ECK Masters light up an event, a dream, or an unusual encounter to clear the way.

They often come in people's dreams, while at other times they offer aid in our daily lives.

The ECK Masters come to teach Souls to hear and see the Sound and Light of God. They lead the inexperienced Soul to self-mastery by awakening love in one's heart.

The ECK Masters help all who really want to find the true love and wisdom that is their divine heritage.

Every one of the great ECK Masters loves people, even as God loves all beings.

*T*o qualify for ECK Mastership, Soul must know discrimination in Its love. Warm love for our dear ones, charity (detached love) for the rest of creation.

*I*s Mastership an attainable goal? Yes, one can become an ECK Master in this life.

The individual must determine to live and act as the ECK Masters do, giving love and service to life in every way imaginable.

It is the real key to living and moving in the highest streams of Light and Sound.

With spiritual liberation comes total freedom and total responsibility.

When you are ready, love, wisdom, and spiritual freedom are available through the teachings of ECK.

About the Author

Author Harold Klemp is known as a pioneer of today's focus on "everyday spirituality." He was raised on a Wisconsin farm and attended divinity school. He also served in the US Air Force.

In 1981, after years of training, he became the spiritual leader of Eckankar, Religion of the Light and Sound of God. His mission is to help people find their way back to God in this life.

Harold Klemp speaks each year to thousands of seekers at Eckankar seminars. Author of more than seventy-five books, he continues to write, including many articles and spiritual-study discourses. Harold Klemp's inspiring and practical approach to spirituality helps thousands of people worldwide find greater freedom, wisdom, and love in their lives.

ALSO BY
HAROLD KLEMP

Available at bookstores, online booksellers,
or directly from:
Eckankar
PO Box 2000, Chanhassen, MN 55317-2000 USA.
Tel (952) 380-2222 Fax (952) 380-2196
www.Eckankar.org

Immortality of Soul Series
The Language of Soul
Love—The Keystone of Life
Truth Has No Secrets
Touching the Face of God
The Awakened Heart
HU, the Most Beautiful Prayer
The Loving Heart

A selected list:
The Call of Soul
The Spiritual Exercises of ECK
The Spiritual Laws of Life
Past Lives, Dreams, and Soul Travel
Those Wonderful ECK Masters